WHO AM I

ANVIL LONG

MENDING A LOST IDENTITY

Anvil Long was devastated to learn he had been conceived during a date rape incident. His lineage, which he had once believed to be an essential element of his being, was lost forever. The pain and internal struggle caused by this revelation consumed his thoughts daily. Anvil found writing helped soothe his suffering. *Who Am I* is a collection of poems and prose that captures his internal feelings as he worked to discover his reimaged identity through the healing process.

Copyright © 2023

CONTENTS

INTRODUCTION   7

PART 1: IMPETUS

BEN LERNER SENT ME HERE   15
I MET SOMEONE   18

PART 2: DISCOVERY

TRUTH   23
FLAWED BY BIRTH   24
WHO AM I?   26
DICHOTOMY   28
THE CLOWN   30
THE OTHER ME   32
SAME DAY   34

PART 3: HEALING

PRAYING FOR NUMBNESS   39
THE DREAM   42

NOT BY BLOOD 44

FINDING MYSELF 46

LEAN WITH THE WIND 48

ALL WE ARE 50

FOCUS 52

THE LAST CHAPTER 54

MY PURPOSE 56

I FORGIVE YOU 57

TUESDAY 58

LIFE GOES ON 60

TODAY A BETTER PLACE 62

LINES 63

ABOUT THE AUTHOR 64

INTRODUCTION

This collection of work was written after learning four "truths".

To begin, let me say that never in my wildest dreams did I ever think I would one day attempt to write poetry or prose. Having it published and subjected to the critique of the literary community—well, that would have just been crazy talk. But life happens. We often get pushed in different directions than the life we had planned for ourselves. This book is a direct result of being pushed. I was pushed very hard as a result of the disclosure of a deep, dark secret. This secret was safely held tight by one person for over 50 years. Learning *the secret* devastated me. I continued to put on a happy face every day for my family, friends, and coworkers, but I was in a strange mental state. My mind was swamped by a fusion of abandonment, depression, and disbelief. For a couple of years there was not a day that went by in which I did not think about my origins and drift into this strange blend of emotions. It was by pure accidental luck that I discovered that the act of writing poetry provides a release from this mental state. This book includes many of these writings; my innermost thoughts, spanning from the time of the *big secret's* revelation to where I am today. To be honest, I know my life will never be as it was prior to learning this secret, but today I don't have to put on a happy face. I *am* happy. I am content. However, I also know I am still recovering from the deep wound to my soul. Only four people on this planet know the *big secret*; my mother, my sister, my wife and, of course, myself. Holding on to *the secret* protects many good and innocent people. There is part of me that wants to share *the secret* with my close friends and relatives; however, the emotional cost would be devastating for too many others who are distantly linked to *the secret*. Publishing this book is a way of sharing *the secret* anonymously and hopefully taking another step forward in the restoration of my spirit.

It was a Thursday evening in May of 2019 when I learned that the man I had always thought to be my father was not my *biological* father; the first "truth". My sister and I thought DNA testing would be fun and introduce us to distant relatives. Unfortunately, we discovered something that neither of us were prepared to learn. My sister turned out to be my *half-sister*. At first, I thought it was no big deal. Since we both had the same mother, it was obvious that the parent that we didn't share was our father. We thought that perhaps my mother had had a brief affair before meeting our father and that I had been con-ceived from this pre-marriage relationship. Or that perhaps my mother had engaged in an affair after I was born which had resulted in my sister's birth. Neither of these scenarios really disturbed me so I decided to not dig any deeper. My father had already passed away a few years earlier. I was very happy holding on to the belief I was his son, and his lineage was my lineage. A lineage with a robust history as told to me by grandparents through many family narratives. I was extremely proud of this lineage, which I believed to be essential to my core being. My sister, however, continued to dig into the matter and within a few weeks she discovered my biological father's name and the names of several of his family members. She informed me that my biological father had passed away a few years earlier, but I had half-siblings through him living in a different state. Learning my biological father's name and the names of my half-siblings was the second "truth". I tried to move on and not think about these family members that I knew in name only, but curiosity eventually overcame me. Late one night, I contacted one of my half-siblings on social media. One thing led to another, and within a few weeks I decided to make the trip to meet my half-siblings and several of their relatives. My newfound relatives seemed eager to embrace me; they had no doubts about my relation to them and welcomed me with hugs and a pot-luck dinner. I was pleased to learn that my half-siblings and their relatives were good people. At that time, I thought I would be accepting of my newfound kinfolk; however, I cannot describe the feelings I experienced—a mixture of awkwardness, detachment, and fear. The next day, I called my sister to tell her about my experience. During this conversation, I mentioned that I was grateful that our dad had already passed away because he hadn't needed to learn that he was not my birth father. There was no doubt in my mind that he had never been aware of the truth. My sister believed that she could reassure me by telling me the third "truth". According to her, when I was two years old, our mom and dad experienced some troubles in their marriage and dad decided to leave our mom. He'd packed his belongings and left, taking me with him. My sister told me that she didn't think our dad would've taken me with him if he'd known I wasn't his biological son—although she was trying to comfort me, the story was painful to hear.

As difficult as the first three "truths" had been to hear, the fourth was the most painful. Along with the other investigations that my sister had undergone, she revealed that she had committed to hounding our mother until she revealed how I came to be. After revealing the third "truth", she went on to tell me that I had not been conceived as a result of a one-night stand or short-lived affair, but that our mother had explained to her that she had been date-raped by a young man that had driven her home from a Saturday night dance. She had never told anyone about this tragic event, including the man who raised me, my father. Our mother had started dating our father soon after the date-rape incident. A few months into this relationship, she found out she was pregnant, and naturally she wanted to believe he was my biological father. It was not until I had submitted myself to DNA testing that she, too, found out the truth. Our mother shared her secret with my sister because she felt she had no choice. Our mother did not expect my sister to tell me the specifics of how I was conceived. I would never have reached out to my biological father's family if I had known how I was conceived. My half-siblings and their families can never know the truth; and if I have anything to do with it, they never will. They do not deserve to feel the anguish I have experienced since learning *the truth*. Logically, I understand that it does not really matter who my biological father is. For me, my father will always be the man who raised me with love, kindness, and compassion. Unfortunately, we cannot always force our brains to think logically and forget everything else. The emotional side of ourselves has a way of monopolizing our thoughts and feelings.

I love my sister, and I know she was trying to help. I'm sure she thought that providing me with this knowledge would somehow make me feel better about my circumstances even though she knew that what she had to share would break my heart and forever change my life. Perhaps it helped her. I often feel that lies would have been better than the truth. I still struggle to accept "how" I was conceived. At first, my solution was to focus on the future and look forward rather than backward, but it turns out that I was wrong to narrow my sights. I learned that my focus couldn't stay solely on the future; that I needed to focus on the good yet to come *and* the good from the past. Everything else was little more than residual baggage. Life can be good, but we need to focus on the good of every day instead of just the potential good of the future.

I was fortunate enough to learn that writing helps me with my struggles. *Who Am I* is a collection of poems and prose; a manifestation of the innermost feelings that were spawned from learning my mother's *big secret*. The exceptions to this are two works in Part One—titled *Impetus*. These writings illuminate the beginning of my journey into writing. The remaining poems chronologically follow my journey from initial hurt to where I am at today. The seven poems in Part Two—*Discovery*—were authored during the time I was at my lowest. This darkness is reflected in the poetry. Part Three—*Healing*—is made up of 14 pieces which were inspired by my progress in healing and rediscovering, or perhaps reinventing, my definition of who I am.

PART ONE

IMPETUS

BEN LERNER SENT ME HERE

Ben Lerner sent me here. I know what you're thinking. Where's this going? Does this guy really know Ben Lerner? Let me explain.

The story begins with a couple of beers at one of my favorite brewpubs. I was talking with my friend Kate, the bartender at a brewpub I frequent. Our conversations run the gamut from senseless to philosophical but are always enjoyable. One evening, Kate mentioned that she likes to read poetry. I wasn't surprised. Kate's certainly cultured and knowledgeable about the arts. I think she was born this way. It's not the same for me. While Kate was telling me about her poem reading, my mind drifted back to my junior year of high school. One of our class assignments required the assembly of a poetry booklet. Selecting and reading a poem from our booklet to the class was also part of the assignment. I can still recite the poem I selected: *Moto,* by Langston Hughes. Amazing how some things just seem to stick with you. But that had been decades ago. I couldn't recall reading any real poetry since those high school years. I wasn't even sure if I wanted to read poetry. My leisure reading for the past few decades had consisted of current events and non-fiction.

I digress. Back to Kate. I asked her the name of her favorite poet. Kate told me she liked several poets, but lately she and her partner liked reading the works of Ben Lerner. Kate used my phone and pushed Ben Lerner's *By Any Measure* towards my face. I'll be honest, I couldn't hold back the laughter as I read this poem out loud. I struggled to find how the words fit together, let alone made any sense. Obviously, I could not see the images the author (and Kate) saw when reading the poem. After I expressed my inability to understand Ben's poem, we quickly went on to the next topic of conversation. A few days passed and for whatever reason, I could not seem to forget Ben's poem. Eventually I admitted to myself that I had not given Ben a fair chance. I looked up some guides on "how to read poetry" and skimmed a couple of articles on the subject. I then found a handful of Ben Lerner's poems. While sitting in solitude, I carefully read through each several times. With a little effort and imagination, I started feeling the emotions and visualizing the poets' images. Over the next few months, I found other poems (and prose) by a variety of authors. I read through this diverse collection. Some I liked, some I *really* liked, and a few I could not seem to grasp. One thing I did learn, however, was that I enjoy reading poetry. Not to dissect and analyze, but for pure enjoyment.

But the next thing that happened is really the best part of this story.

Recalling that I had told Kate that anyone could throw words onto a page and call it poetry, I decided to write a few lines and give them to Kate—as a joke. Here's the crazy part: when I started trying to draft a lighthearted, corny poem to give to Kate, my mind went someplace else. It jumped to hidden memories and emotions. I felt compelled to put my innermost thoughts on paper. The more I typed, the better I felt. Authoring poetry turned out to be very pleasurable, relaxing, and even therapeutic for me. I now look forward to having a few hours of alone time to sit down and put my thoughts into words. It does not matter that some might find my words primitive and only meaningful to me. It does not matter that my writings will not be read by more than a handful of people. It does not even matter that my own family and friends will never read my work or compliment my efforts. I write for myself. I write for the satisfaction it gives me. I write to exhale the emotions that I previously kept suppressed. Maybe at some point my writings will be considered publishable. Or maybe not.

No matter. I still plan to keep putting words on paper—for my benefit if for no other reason. Without Ben Lerner, I would not have come to this point. Yes, Ben sent me to this place. A place that I do not want to leave. Thank you, Ben Lerner. And thank you to Kate, the muse who granted me inspiration, kindness, and clarity; more than I ever gave back. I am grateful.

I MET SOMEONE
(My Muse)

I met Someone

Who I find quite charming—
Not reciprocal I am sure
At least not from the beginning

I find this person moving
They make me reflect further than most;
Not wanting to end the duologue
But anxious to start the next

The judgement's not logical at times
But always on the principled path
Keen to make the world better
Grasping for resolve together

I find myself granting openings
Conflicting with my expected silence
Regarding my alternate existences,

Imparting bygone scars, revealing future longings

Easy without restraint—
Transgressing both decency and debauchery
Deeds from ancient episodes
And possibilities for chapters to come

The banter makes me smile
And returns me to primitive places
Dreams reawaken
Inevitability suddenly buds with promise

Our measure together is precise
Not continually certain
Who knows when, but it will be broken.

PART TWO

DISCOVERY

TRUTH
(Why Tell Me)

The truth must always be spoken:
From childhood we are charged.

But is it really what is best?
When truth wounds without end,
When truth cannot be wrenched back.

Yes, it was I who sanctioned the unmasking,
Unconscious of the anguish the disclosing would bear.
The skeleton, revealed with good intent,
Severed my lineage, erased my identity,
Whittled away my core and rendered me much less than
before.
Now I walk each day,
Afflicted with the *Truth* etched into my being.

FLAWED BY BIRTH

I was born flawed
Formed not from love nor mutual longing
But from pain and guilt that fill the silent places

Can I become whole?
Or will I forever be branded lesser
Destined to a life of inadequacy

No matter how hard I try
Serenity evades me as I walk among the righteous
Keeping my secret and professing to be simple

Fearful others will eventually see
But more afraid of keeping the secret inside
In a place that no one can reach

How do I move onwards
Knowing my starting point was not meant to be
But forced upon my life giver without regret

And bearing me, flawed forevermore
Perhaps one day I can confess how I surfaced
And show the scars that tell my story for all to see

When this day comes
Will the doubt and anxiety inside me disappear?
Will the righteous judge me no different knowing of my
beginning?

Or will the anguish only spread
When the wounds are opened for all bloodlines to see?
This greater ache clutches reality tightly inside

Time does not heal all wounds
Some secrets should never be revealed
This trueness, infinitely my destiny.

WHO AM I?

In a faraway place
Where I find myself viewing life play on
Not understanding the spoken words that reach my ear
Nor recognizing the forms that shuffle about

In between the passing hours
A white-haired man appears
Breaking the babble with a familiar declaration
And passing time with restful chat

Then came his interrogation:
Where are your roots, what blood runs through your veins?
Lost answers that once were beyond debate
Before gene examination expunged my authenticity

The foundation of my being,
That which had created me and pulled me forward each day,
Suddenly jerked away without hope of return
Today my identity cannot be voiced

Complexities strain my presence.
Is the folklore that made me
And pointed to the beginnings of my circle
Still embedded in my soul?

Will I learn the mysteries of my existence?
Unveil unknown chronicles, define myself anew?
Or will I forever be partially erased,
Destined to a life without depth?

I elect not to seek the answers
For fear of what I may expose
My path forward may be burdensome
But at some point, I'll emerge complete

Looking back to the white-haired man
Returning his queries with my balm:
Sir, my roots run deep, and my blood runs true
This I know, for it is reckoned to be so.

DICHOTOMY
(Intrinsically Human)

Since the beginning

I stumbled from heaven
>Yet ascended from hell

Light guided my steps
>Yet darkness steered me astray

Oxygen suffused my being
>Yet space stifled my breath

Crowds surrounded me
>Yet solitary was my existence

Tranquility was my comfort
>Yet chaos was all I could hear

Devotion galvanized my philosophy
>Yet fear dampened my prospects

Self-assurance filled my presence
        Yet I could not escape distrust

Liberty was my destiny
        Yet oppression was my constant

Ecstasy was within my touch
        Yet suffering was all I could reach

Is this all there is?

THE CLOWN

You see him,
But do you really see him?
He paints on a smile or maybe a frown
His hat does not fit and his shoes are too big
We laugh and we laugh

Chasing bubbles, puffing up balloon animals
Throwing seven balls high in the air
Riding one wheel in circles
We laugh and we laugh

What is the clown thinking?
His surface does not tell us
Does it not matter?
We laugh and we laugh

Will we ever recognize him?
Be there for him when he is sad,
Celebrate with him when he is happy?
We laugh and we laugh

We know only what he flaunts
Beyond we are not allowed to grasp
Do we like him? Do we hate him?
We laugh and we laugh

What is the clown feeling?
His surface does not tell us
Does it not matter?
We laugh and we laugh

His countenance, not forthright
His veil, an impassable shield
Our lens purposefully blurred
We laugh and we laugh

Will the clown someday cease to be?
Will the bona fide side one day emerge?
Or will his eulogy only proclaim
We laughed and we laughed?

THE OTHER ME

I see him—
He cannot see me. Or perhaps he does not recognize me.

He's the one who everyone likes.
He's smart, seems so confident, certainly accomplished

Why does he glance over to me from time to time?
I am a nobody, not worthy of his gaze

I dream about being him
And sometimes I'll pretend.

But people know that I am not him
They say nothing, just being nice. They know I am not him.

Maybe if I rehearse over and over again
I could become him—or at least resemble him

No doubt people will still know the truth:
I could never be him.

If I pretend to be him
People will find out. "Pretender" written on my nametag

Why do I want to be him?
Is it the connection? Is it the expectation? Is it the affirma-
tion?

How did I get to this place?
Why try to be someone that I am not?

Could it be the real me is not what I wanted?
Or worse, not what the world wants?

I will never be him
But I will never stop trying.

The life of an imposter...
We have no choice
We can never be
Who the world believes us to be.

Today is the same
Yesterday was forever ago
Tomorrow will never come
From my window, I watch the snowfall
Still, the white will not cover my darkness

Today is the same
My daydreams never changing
Always drifting back to the hurt
I can hear tunes that soothe my soul
Still, the melody cannot erase my pain

Today is the same
I sit alone thinking of the past
Was it a lie or just a wish
Everyone and no one have the answers
Still, I know not the truth

Today is the same
I am not seen as I walk the streets

My name is never called
I meet my reflection in the mirror
Still, I don't know who I am

HEALING

PRAYING FOR NUMBNESS

healing
the process of becoming sound.
can this be done when
the dagger that caused my identity to be severed
cannot be pulled out.

when
the blood that created and
sustained my being
will never be restored,
never ring true.

does
an antidote exist
for such a venom
as hurtful and permanent
as the loss of self?

can
healing remove

the longing for pedigree?
alleviate the misery
of a lost soul?

perhaps
healing in the truest sense
is not the answer.
the cost would
be too great.

perhaps
the still-wounded Self,
albeit agonizing, will keep
the folk tales alive
for all witnesses to judge.

veiling
the truth, protecting
loved ones from torment.
regrettably this, without doubt,
is the only remedy.

deep
in my core
suffering continues to live.
emotions remain internal,
forever keep me burdened.

healing
does not exist for me

although numbness would be divine,
empowering a corridor forward
sanctioning an ordinary life.

numbness
I pray, will come swiftly,
as numbness,
you see, is my only liberator.

THE DREAM

I frequently dream when I sleep. There is no rhyme or reason to the content of my dreams, it ranges from the insane to the mundane. But all my dreams tend to be very clear and vivid; while I dream and for a few seconds after first awakening, I find it hard to distinguish them from reality. Soon after waking, however, the details of my dreams vanish, dissolving into nothing more than blurred images which hang around for a few days before fading from my memory. I have never believed that my dreams meant anything. In them I've found no hidden messages, no prophetic revelations. I see my nightmare imaginings as silly dreams sparked as my brain worked to clear the fog. I used to think that if I concentrated on a specific image or experience as I fell asleep, they might influence my dreaming; but it has never worked.

My dreaming patterns changed notably for a few years after I learned the *big secret*. I did not notice this at first, but after a few months, I realized I was no longer dreaming at night, or at least I did not remember any of my dreams. I attributed this change to not being able to sleep well. It was in the still of the night when my mind most often drifted to the *big secret*. I could not help but think about my existence, my origins, and how my father would have treated me if he had known. My mind often took me to places where I did not want to be.

Eventually a dream did come to me. This dream was different than the others in that I could remember the most minute details for longer than for just a few seconds after I woke. In fact, I can still clearly remember this dream. I was standing alone in a meadow. My father was slowly walking toward me. He soon reached me and said, *I know. It's okay. I love you.* My father then hugged me and kissed me on my forehead. That was it. Only three short sentences and a kiss. A simple dream, yet it filled me with a huge sense of liberation. Perhaps this dream was some sort of coping mechanism my mind had summoned. Or maybe, it was my father's spirit talking to me. The logical explanation is that deep inside me, I knew precisely what my father would tell me if he was still living. Ultimately, it doesn't matter if the dream was some mystic experience or if it was my logical thoughts finally falling into place as I slept. All that matters is that from that point on, I felt different. I felt better. I knew I was going to be okay. Yes, I still have thoughts of lost identity, but not as often as before, and these thoughts are now short-lived. I started sleeping soundly again. Thankfully, the random crazy dreams came back as well. My healing started with this dream and continues today. I know I will get there one day—thanks to my father, who raised me, loved me, and came to me in a dream to tell me exactly what I needed to hear.

NOT BY BLOOD

Connected by blood
>people proudly proclaim
>as if their relationship is much stronger
>for the mutual blood flowing through their veins

They have the same blood
>another phrase I quite often hear
>when comparisons are craved
>to correlate personas, justify emotions

My blood is your blood
>a father holding his newborn tight
>whilst imagining mini-me futures
>quietly whispers this into his ear

Yet I ask, is it the blood that cements our union?
>or provides love unconditionally
>forever protecting, forever bolstering
>sharing both pain and joy

No, no, no, I answer. It's not the blood that binds us
        or recognizes our cry in a crowd
        or sees the trouble in our face
        or senses our need from afar

It is the nurturing that binds us together
        stronger than the kinship that links
        stronger than the love that evokes
        stronger than the DNA that authenticates

My father, not by blood,
        cultivated me since the beginning
        directed my shaping, hardened my edge
        and truly created my being

The bond between us
        first tied at my birth
        preserved through ups and downs of the seasons
        still endures beyond the grave

Nurturing in my equation
        cannot be denied
        for my father, not by genetics,
        could not have been grander
        could not have loved greater
        could not be loved further
        my father, not by blood

FINDING MYSELF
(Motorbikes)

Motorbikes: why do I ride?

Solitude
yes, I ride alone, this is nice, but
there is something more

Freedom
no question that I feel liberated, but
there is something else

Power
the feeling of power is awesome, but
there is something further

Individualism
call me a maverick, but
there is still something beyond
I take the paths that others tend to pass over.

Most like twisting roads and travel in packs.
Not for me—I like long, straight desolate roads, solo.
Out west is best
Where you can ride for hours without being too bothered by
civilization.

I see desert, tall grass prairies, and high plains wilderness.
I see for miles and miles.
I see no people.
I hear the wind. I hear the engine grumble.
If I am lucky, I can hear the cracks in the roadway belting out
a rhythm.
I hear distant tunes playing in my head.
Amid these rides, I find the calm. I find the missing frag-
ments.
I find myself.
I ride and I ride until I put down my bedroll under the stars.
Crickets, coyotes, and hoot owls sing me to sleep.
Tomorrow I will ride.
I will ride—and I will find myself.
Yes, I will ride and ride until I put down my bedroll under the
stars.
Crickets, coyotes, and hoot howls will sing me to sleep.
And again,
I will find myself.

LEAN WITH THE WIND

Whoever said, "lean into the wind"
Has not gazed upon a solitary cottonwood
Standing resolute on the high plains prairie
Stubbornly weathering the passing decades

The resilient cottonwood
Grasps that lasting existence
In this taxing space can be reached only
Through leaning *with* the wind, not *into*

Tilting ever so slightly with the constant gusts
Giving a little, yet flourishing despite
Allowing the wind to gracefully pass
Without fight, without burden

The wind rewards the cottonwood
For this conciliation by carrying the
Cottonwood's offspring afar
Ensuring survival beyond forever

The wind and the cottonwood
On the high plains prairie
Each has a place, each has a charge
Working as one, both living their destiny

Perhaps I too shall lean with the wind
Not fight my darkness
Not burden my circle
Gracefully living with the ache
To find stillness within my soul

ALL WE ARE

all we are is

a collection of experiences
       from our beginnings, tough to summon the lot
       but they are inside of us; the good, the bad, the indif-
ferent
       rolling around, paying no attention to time or place
       only halting for brief moments of recall
       before receding back to concealed position

a collection of thoughts
       changing with our seasons, changing with our state
       deep, shallow, convergent, divergent, creative, sexual,
abstract
       does not matter—a thought is a thought
       most drift off course and fail to right
       but all are fleeting by life's measure

a collection of feelings
       formed from our place of humanity

trust, surprise, anticipation, happiness,
disgust, jealousy, loneliness, anger, sadness,
and those who are lucky, or perhaps have suffered
more,
have discovered their capacity to domesticate

a collection of connections
which link us to society, link us to our meaning
through love, friendship, blood, or hatred
by choice, by consequence, or by force
strong, weak, and passing
evolving with time, ceaseless until death

all we are
is this distinctive collection
that defines our beings
imparts our foundations
assigns our symmetries
renders us exclusive

we are no more, we are no less
even so, we are
. . . until we are not

FOCUS

Focus — can it be that simple

silence in the darkness of night
is the hardest
my mind spins off course; thoughts that should not awaken
focus — tomorrow, life will be good

triggers explode during awkward stretches
explanations eternally an enigma
pictures in my head; images that cannot be discarded
focus — tomorrow, life will be good

casual quizzes from faultless speakers
begging to be satisfied
two performances endure; actuality won't be spoken
focus — tomorrow, life will be good

in solitude, as life carries on
abandonment creeps in
inner doubts linger; remedies perpetually denied

focus — tomorrow, life will be good
lingering, concentrated contemplation
the substance of my mind
morphs to blameless form; hopeful future and contented past
focus — yesterday and tomorrow, life is good and will be
good

it is not that simple, it is work — but it is *Focus* that makes life
good

THE LAST CHAPTER

Each writes their own volume
Pages of life for all to witness
With the last chapter absent
Awaiting other's hands to inscribe

Some are storybook—
Perfect beginnings, predictable ends
Genre both joyous and tragic

Few with plots intwined and tangled
Riddles dotted inside and out
Beckoning, prodding, for what may be freed
Most are simple and mundane
Like the milk maid pouring milk from her earthen jug
A lifetime of stillness, fashioned through humbly persisting
Dreadful, the breathing to never know their finale
For only after death will the last chapter be penned
The ending as one lived, and *not* as one devised

As the final digest is chiseled onto the pages of one's existence
Will life as pictured meet the life lived?
Will memories of the soul warmly fade with the setting sun?

Will links be kind, forgiving, and gaze beyond the failings?
Or will one's acts bear a chronicle that can never be gently
received?

MY PURPOSE

I often wonder. No; I often question:
Is my purpose being satisfied?

If my purpose is to make a difference. A difference to some-
one, to something, to the world we call home.
How do I know I am?

If my purpose is to connect, to be part of a community, to
love and to be loved.
How do I know I am?

If my purpose is to fulfill some random sequence, a hap-
hazard series of complex events, a casting of lots—to only
survive, to only breathe for as long as I can gasp air, to only
live for as long as my physical body exists
Why would I care?
Because I care, I must have purpose.
Perhaps one day
My purpose will appear

I FORGIVE YOU

I forgive you. Three words, eleven letters. Should be easy to utter and even easier to hear. Yet, they will go unsaid when needed most. Is it too much focus on the hurt, not the cure? Too much pride and not enough caring? Too many wrongs, not enough attempts to heal? Perhaps too many excuses for every circumstance.

Forgiveness can repair the broken, soothe the vexed, and free the soul. Still, forgiveness remains elusive for both the offender and the offended. Without absolution, the wound will fester and widen the divide. And with time, it is the "not forgiving" that becomes the greater hurt.

Perhaps if forgiveness would erase the memories, then forgiveness would always come quick, always be sincere, and always purge the pain. But it is the memory that triggers the torture and builds the wall. Yes, I can forgive, but the memory remains. And it is the memory that keeps us apart.

Love has not diminished. Forgiveness was never in question. But the distance fogs the memory and so lessens the pain.

TUESDAY
(Inspirations for a Day)

Yawning,
Today is Tuesday
Fresh brewed coffee
Sipping the sensations

Sun rising
Blossoming red and orange
Warming the body
Fostering anticipation

Passing jogger
Pulling the master
Leashed golden retriever
Panting with laughter

Early morning drive
Classic oldies blaring
Sparking ancient memories
Here ever after
Schoolkids' bus stop

Yakking, laughing, playing
Eager to discover
Innocence gushing

Out in the park
Three old men
Practicing Tai Chi
Slow, methodical, mesmerizing

Fresh baked muffin
Hovering aroma indisputable
Lump of butter melting
Utterly irresistible

Friends at a pub
Socializing, philosophizing, strategizing
Always cherishing
Reluctantly departing

Sun setting
Fading purple and scarlet
Relaxing distant melody
Resting, contemplating, absorbing

Inspiration dissolves
But fresh are soon forthcoming
Yawning,
Tomorrow is Wednesday

Open heart, open mind, inspiration springs eternal.

LIFE GOES ON

We are all unique. Each of us has our own set of catastrophes, our own set of triumphs. Some of us are better off, some are worse off; in wealth, health, experiences, and birthright. In our world, equality and innocence belong only to children. The equilibrium of our existence is founded on unremitting change. For good, for bad, but constant. Our lives are just a blip on the timeline. Ticking to a timepiece we cannot stop or reset. Things happen and will happen. Each day carries on and we wake to live within a world that we seek to escape. More effort is wasted on having things and being entertained than loving and being loved.

We have lost the ability to balance the rights of the individual with the rights of the population. We have lost the understanding of who is our neighbor. We elect leaders who have no integrity, no gallantry, no compassion, no ability to find middle ground. We call ourselves civilized but accept being uncivilized. We all ache for utopia, but we cannot agree what utopia is or how we get there.

Too many of us are oblivious to the wrongs in our world. We ignore what we do not understand. We justify the unjustifiable when it aligns with our biases. We seek to live only in a circle that mirrors ourselves and we fear those beyond. We press all who don't fit our paradigms to conform to our ideals. We do not recognize individuality and inclusivity, nor do we accept them. We pick, decrypt, and mutate even our religions to vindicate our failings.

One can choose to capitulate. Live as a casted cog in this undying machine. Or we can embrace Charles Bukowski's counsel:

> *"We are here to unlearn the teachings of the church, state, and our educational system. We are here to drink beer. We are here to kill war. We are here to laugh at the odds and live our lives so well that Death will tremble to take us."*

Do not judge, not hate, not exclude. Understand and accept. Always seek wisdom, live humbly, and honor all humanity. Survive each day like it's the last. And drink beer.

Yes, life goes on.

How one wants to live and how one does live can be far apart. To unite this divide is my steadfast end.

TODAY A BETTER PLACE

I have learned much in the past few years. About myself.

I have learned family is not defined by blood, it is not defined by paper certificates, and certainly not defined by a tree of lines. Family is who I choose. A choice based on love, on commitment, on mutual acceptance.

I am callous towards my heritage. My curiosity of distant relatives has waned. My faith in pedigree, as defined on paper, has been erased.

I now know I am who I am, not because of lineage, folklore, or tradition, but because of choice. I fashion myself into who I am. I decide. Nothing is predestined.

The pain of knowing the truth has lessened. I am very close to numbness after taking all that I could hope to endure.

I embrace these newfound realities. I am in a much better place. I believe my way of thinking has been enriched and my acceptance of humanity has broadened. I am nearer to discovering my purpose. For this, I am thankful.

LINES

Blood lines, family lines, no lines

Blood lines define our pedigree.
Perhaps important for dogs, horses, bluebloods, and their
wannabes.
But do blood lines make us who we are?

Family lines define our connections.
Those we love, cherish, trust, and lend our time.
But do family lines make us who we are?

No lines make us who we are.
We are what we make of ourselves.
Shaped by experiences, tugged at by our thoughts, revealed by
our actions

Erasing the *who am I?*
Stating the *who I am.*
Only then, will we be.

ABOUT THE AUTHOR

Anvil Long spent too many years making life happen, living and working in many different cities in the US, Europe, and Pacific Rim. Now Anvil lets life happen. You will find him somewhere in the Midwest where he enjoys his solitude riding motorcycles and frequenting quiet brewpubs. Anvil, an expert spectator of nature and people, is always searching for wisdom. Writing is Anvil's therapy and his way of passing along his questions, and perhaps an occasional answer.